MODERN SUTRAS FROM NURSES

Finding Peace

AUTHORS AND CO-EDITORS

JEAN WATSON
& SEAN M. REED

LOTUS
LIBRARY

LOTUS
LIBRARY

Watson Caring
Science Institute

Table of Contents

Background

This 'sutra' project emerged from an intensive Watson Caring Science Institute Course offered by Dr. Jean Watson in 2020 and 2021. It is structured as a series of personal 'sutra' messages as an entrée or 'way shower' toward modern veritas-caritas spiritual consciousness for self-growth and inner truth for more meaningful spirit-filled life.

Sutras, both ancient and contemporary, serve as spiritual teachings of human-divine awakening. The origin of the word sutra comes from 'suture' or 'sew'; to bring together, to mend, to hold together, reminders of greater truths beyond the outer world. In Sanskrit, the word *sutra* means 'thread' to bind together ideas, serving as a guide or protector to adhere to holy steps on the sacred path toward enlightenment, beyond ego. In other words, sutras serve as a kind of handbook guiding an individual toward a meaningful life connected to a higher power, source of consciousness.

This collection of sacred sutras, for and from nurses and health professionals, is evoked as a spirit-filled metaphoric project, as an entrée, a mantra, to deep self-surrender for sacred healthcare caring-healing service, beyond self. Rather, a realization that we are all One; each authors' sutra reflects an awakening of our 'Unity of being, belonging, and becoming' to the cosmic universal sacred circle of infinite love.

This awakening leads toward a realization that "I am You; You are Me." I am one with nature and all universal living things. By evoking a sutra we suture or thread together all within the infinite, non-physical, spirit-filled plane with unbounded consciousness, sharing the essence of Human-Divine Mother/Father Sky Cosmic Oneness.

Sutras point toward enduring truths of our divinity — honoring the perennial human search for The Beloved. The concept of a sutra converges with the Greek meaning of the term *'Veritas'* – enduring, universal, timeless, eternal truths (Watson, 2021), which are posited as foundational to the moral ethical value covenant nursing has with society. Veritas underpins transpersonal caring and caritas (caring-healing and infinite cosmic love) timeless values for sustaining our divinity (Watson, 1985, 1999, 2008, 2018).

In viewing modern versions of sutras developed by nurses and health professionals, please view them as guides and pointers on our shared higher-self journey, hopefully helping us all to identify and engage spirit-filled truisms to ground and elevate Watson's Unitary Caring Science as sacred science. As such, this collection of modern Veritas sutras invites and calls forth an evolutionary path toward unitary sacred consciousness for Veritas-Caritas Practices — for self/other/nature/Divine Mother/our Universe.

In this modern Veritas sacred sutra project, the individual sutras from each author can serve as a mantra for sacred heart practices, thus evoking a spiritual awakening of Watson's Unitary Caring Science as truly a sacred science, requiring personal-professional spiritual evolution as essential to healing/holy Caritas praxis; an opening up to the full depth of divine, infinite love, transcendence (Watson, 2018).

Introduction

Sacred Sutras

Sacred sutras, more formally, are brief aphoristic compositions of Ancient Hindu teachings — the way of spiritual elders; highly laden energetic words or phrases that point to spiritual truths, source, spirit as ancient truth teachings. Sutras can serve as a prayer or breaths of quietude of the busy mind. Sutras are basic forms of almost all ancient religions such as Hinduism and Buddhism and of early Indian philosophers who did not work with written texts. Sutras were memorized, chanted and recited for thousands of years and to this day as a way toward enlightenment and higher God consciousness, transcending self and outer world (Watson, 2021, 2022).

Sutras in nursing

Sutras in nursing can serve as ancient universal wisdom truths to live and evolve by, uniting with universal truths and universal love consciousness for caring and healing. Celebrating and embracing 'Source' as universal love consciousness — Caritas Consciousness — as a guide to self-other healing, acknowledging energy of love as the highest level of consciousness and greatest source for all healing.

Watson's Unitary Caring Science, and Era III

Unitary transformative thinking extends our understanding of nursing. Watson's Caring Science, and Transpersonal Caring, resides within a unitary field of consciousness (Watson, 2018). This paradigmatic evolution of theory and science has been acknowledged as the most mature nursing paradigm to accommodate nursing's human phenomena of wholeness, caring, health, presence, pattern, consciousness, spirit-energy, and so on (Cowling et al., 2008; Newman et al., 2008; Smith, 1999, 2013; Watson, 2008, 2018, 2021).

Timeless, core, eternal, lasting values that nursing honors as universal for moral practice are referred to as Veritas (Watson, 2018). Raising new questions: What is important? What matters? And what is lasting and timeless beyond the current moment of crisis and fear?

Numerous philosophical, scientific treatises, and writings about knowledge and science across time remind us that teachings from the world's greatest saints, yogis, and sages were about another kind of living and being — another form of "discipline." Now here in post-pandemic existential time, we open to an inner-disciplinary knowing — that which emerges from within, inviting inner and outer alignment for Veritas (core timeless values) Healing (*qua* Holy) Praxis. This sanctions a human-spirit awakening; beyond the material knowledge of the rational-cognitive-ego world. This other world is spirit-energy, non-physical and trans-rational, beyond knowing, to "no-knowing-not knowing" a form of hidden primordial knowing, available to anyone, seeking deep truth (Watson, 2019,p. 62). These congruent disciplinary practices open up sacred space for a wise knowing of self as spirit, disclosing the shadow-light on our shared humanity — awakening to the truth or falsity of alignment with higher self/soul/source.

Timeless Veritas — Lasting Truth

Ig/nor/ance of one's true self, or being preoccupied with outer-world turbulence, generates more fear and suffering, leading to more and more upheaval. This very material, physical outer-world dilemma begs for an introspective, existential shift, a search for the sacred, for the spiritual, toward meaningful, self-consoling contemplative practices — seeking Veritas: inner truth, which is timeless, lasting and evolving in graceful divine flow (Watson, 2018).

The existential-spiritual Veritas awakening after experiencing outer chaos marks a higher consciousness, spiraling upward and downward in alignment — serving as an inner guide and "way shower" for compassion, strength, purpose, meaning, and creative insights. Veritas invites stillness and silence, to go within, releasing, repatterning, the all-encompassing, global field of fear, isolation, sensory and touch deprivation; loss, grief, death and dying and all in-between.

We now come face-to-face with self-true inner self.

It is here in the quantum shift from outer physical to inner spirit-filled, infinite field of universal cosmic love that we embrace the sacred life/death cycles as one. It is here with this deep turn, dedicated to a new form of disciplined Veritas practices, that we access the existential, the ineffable, opening to the holy, the sacred, the wonder, the miraculous. We await and expect/accept sacred "creative emergence" (Smith, 1999) as we open to infinite possibilities — approaching Chardin's "Omega Point" God/divine love consciousness.

The wisdom teachings of Joseph Campbell identified different disciplinary steps toward self-growth that help us to transcend and transition from outer to inner self/world. They include being and belonging as One consciousness; evolving to higher vibrational consciousness; and connecting with field of cosmic-infinite love — these are all other ways to "follow your bliss," and experience joy, wonder, rapture, beauty, grace, divine, miracles — within and without.

Nursing Sutras — Caritas/Veritas Self-Evolution

Watson, 2018, p. 2022

All caring, sacred science holistic practitioners can draw upon each other's sacred sutras as growth work toward Caritas-Veritas spiritual alignment for professional Caritas Consciousness evolution. We practice who we are; we research who we are; we teach who we are; and we live who we are. So, our very being/becoming/belonging more human and humane is what is at stake in sacred caring-healing work. Such holistic practices of deepening our humanity requires a form of deep, self-caring discipline in small and grand ways. All traditions and cultures around the world have ways to enter sacred spiritual practices. Traditional practices across diverse cultures unite in exercising some form of prayer-meditation; fasting; ceremonies; rituals; acts of worship; celebration; acts of simplicity, solitude — all forms of self-discipline, dedicated to deep personal practice. Nevertheless, there are endless ways to enter the inner kingdom. As Rumi put it:

"There are a thousand ways to kneel and kiss the ground."

As we transition during this time to a higher order toward our true divine self, non-physical/nonrational, non-local consciousness, spirit-guided ways, we are helped to find a new grounding to move forward. Each of the so-called spiritual/religious rituals, mantras, sutra practices require self-discipline, commitment, patterns, even rituals, to help us embrace greater dimensions to human existence, beyond the body-material physical. These common ways to approach the sacred and the holy invite us to the transpersonal paradox of "Now Presence;" Whitehead's "Eternal Now," present to the here-and-now, while simultaneously transcending the ego-time present. Dropping into "Being-in-the-moment," becomes a gift to self — a graceful, self-disciplinary holistic practice to advance our relation to everything else. This ability to transcend to cosmic source consciousness, through authentic stillness presence, opens us to an infinity universe — liberates, clears, and opens the higher consciousness field where we are not only connected with source — we are One with all.

Personal Sacred Sutras

WAY - SHOWERS TO VERITAS/CARITAS CONSCIOUSNESS

The next section of this collection of sutras from nurses and health professionals is offered as a Veritas Sutra Guide which may be helpful to each of us in our own way. Moreover, these sutra collections may call you to share your own sutras as we collectively evolve together to a higher dimension as sacred activism for self, shared humanity, and our planet Earth.

Jean's Seven Sutras

Stillness

Silence

Solitude

Spirit

Simplicity

Service

Surrender

Finding Our Sutras

Sean M. Reed

My Journey Finding Sacred Sutras

Introduction

The sacred work I've been doing for the past 17 years has brought me to an awakening. When Jean Watson introduced her Seven Sacred Sutras, she shared that they were her brief prayers and practice to face herself: "To stop the mind; breathe every breath a prayer; to open to unknowns and mysteries; to bow in awe, gratitude and devotion to the beyond" (Watson, 2021, p. 4). I could not help but wonder what my own sacred sutras might be.

Sutras are described by Watson (2021) as energetically laden words or phrases that point to spiritual truths. A sutra is a type of compass that points to inner knowing and universal wisdom by connecting the vibration of words and phrases to ancient truths. While the sutra points the way, it is not the facet itself. Here I will share with you my journey and reflection of discovering my own sacred sutras.

Release — in silence, let go and welcome the holy

My story begins with my first day in doctoral education.

Jean Watson. The professor in my class. What an amazing opportunity for an early-career nurse. I waited — we all waited — sitting in a square, in a classroom, quiet, grinning. I remember exactly the moment when Jean walked in with a Tibetan singing bowl. Jean said that as she tapped the bowl with a wooden striker, we should close our eyes and center. I had never centered myself before a class. The class, this kind of space, was not a centering center. But this dedicated act of mindfulness, on this day, with these people, in this place, resonated. Letting go of the outside chatter in our mind, letting go of the worries and distractions, allowing a time of peacefulness, calm, and allowance for the holy to be authentically present. At the time, I felt these actions allowed me to cast off counter-productive clutter and connect with the momentous, numinous eternal; as I reflect now, I feel that by taking those actions, on that specific day, I started to formulate a sutra: release.

As I continued through my doctoral education, I became a master learner of Watson's Caring Science and took additional courses with Jean. As a bedside nurse at the Veterans Affairs medical center, I began to write specialized nursing notes based on Watson's (2005) Caritas Processes® and created a section in each note about what specific caring practices I engaged in with my patient. I recall a fellow nurse once asked me, "Hey, why do you write that stuff in your note?" I smiled and replied, "Because I want to give voice and evidence of human caring…and I hope you will, too." It was a powerful moment as we were looking at each other eye to eye. Weeks went by and I began to see my colleague and other nurses on the unit adding elements of the Caritas Processes in their own nursing notes. I valued caring theory and became an advocate for Watson's Caring Science. Along the way, even as I kept collecting notes and elements that improved both my academic and clinical selves, I never forgot to release all the stuff that had become obsolete and was weighing me down.

Values — clarity in what is important

Then, I entered my dissertation phase.

I became a mentee of Marlaine Smith. It was during this time that I began to explore and learn Martha Rogers' Science of Unitary Human Beings. An exploration of Rogers' work is nothing if not mind-expanding and paradigm-exploding: Marlaine helped me understand the worldview underpinning unitary caring science, and she guided me as I constructed a new, more expansive personal theoretical foundation. I advanced my nursing career as a palliative care clinical nurse specialist, and my practice was guided by unitary caring theory. As part of my own doctoral development, I worked with Marlaine in developing a theory of healing through touch from a unitary caring lens (Smith & Reed, 2007; 2008) and later published a unitary caring conceptual model for advanced practice nursing in palliative care (Reed, 2010). My dissertation study focused on interviews of participants who provided and received massage or simple touch near the end of life. I analyzed and interpreted the interviews through a unitary caring approach (Reed, 2011), and it would be years later that I actually published the providers' experiences (Reed et al., 2021). I came to realize that every single one of my actions — from the biggest, most significant career undertaking to the smallest, most commonplace daily choice — had to be driven by, infused with, and emblematic of all the principles I hold most dear. Through these realizations and practices, I found another sutra: values.

After I graduated, I continued to work for the largest health care system in Colorado. I developed advanced practice registered nurse models of palliative care in the acute, post-acute, and ambulatory settings — I continued my work in caring science through practical, tangible application. In reflection, doing this work aligned with my values and beliefs. So I created seminars and training sessions focused on unitary caring approaches to patient care. I even implemented a quality improvement project for enhancing patient/ family satisfaction called Preventable Suffering using Halldorsdottir's (1991) five basic modes of being as the theoretical model. This project was disseminated in the acute and post-acute settings, and especially, in home health and hospice care. As a leader in the system, I routinely utilized the grounding and centering technique I had learned years before from

Jean. I began a tradition of early morning prayer, blessing and forgiving the system I worked in, and I strived to be the best I could be, but I was not taking care of myself. I did not realize until later that I had closed myself off from the universe and was hurting.

Love — unconditional gratitude, honor, blessing, forgiveness of others. Grace — forgiveness of self

Next, I left my organization and took a few years off to travel. During this time, I performed a lot of introspection and discovered aspects of myself I had not known existed. I traveled alone to Australia, parts of the US, and all over Europe. I made new friends, developed short and long-term relationships, and rediscovered myself. I explored different practices in spirituality and learned what values were important to me. I reconnected with my spirit and my heart, and I began to heal. I reconnected with my family and strengthened relationships that had been fading. I believe through this entire process I became more open to receiving love into my life, and towards the end of my "sabbatical", in Romania, I met Andrei, who later was to become my husband.

I began to view the Caritas Processes through a different lens. I had always considered the processes to be a way of being with others; suddenly, I was seeing the Caritas Processes as a way of universal belonging. So, I worked purposefully to articulate my values and beliefs in prayer rituals, especially in the morning to begin my day. And I still do this: I kneel facing the east, metaphorically viewing the rising sun. I use a prayer pillow to remind me to ground myself in Mother Earth. I close my eyes, with my hands on my lap, and say,

"I am taking this time and I am influencing the caritas field. I have a full complement of knowledge and understanding, and I am a safe and loving person… and I bow to the holy."

I bow, return to the kneeling position, and say,

"I believe in the tenets of expanding conscience, higher learning, and education. Each moment in my day is a learning opportunity. I am mindful of my thoughts, energy, and actions and recognize I am not alone and that we are all one. With each encounter, I have an open mind respecting the other where they are in that time, space, and place… and I bow to the holy."

I bow, return to the kneeling position, and say,

"I believe in the tenet of spiritual discipline. That I may remember to keep this ritual and moment in

*prayer every day. I am grateful for the encounters
and experiences that I have and for those I create.
I approach each engagement with loving kindness,
forgive those who may hurt me for they know not what
they do. I bless you [name of person who comes to mind]
and forgive you. I bless and forgive myself recognizing
that I too am human. I believe we are all one in unity
and recognize my thoughts, energy, and actions are
connected to the cosmos. I recognize love and caring
are the basis for universal healing. I love you [name of
person], and I love myself… and I bow to the holy."*
I bow, return to the kneeling position, and say,

*"I believe in the tenet of perfect health. Mind-body-
spirit unified as one with the environment. Light
surrounds me and expands, filling space…it continues
outward expanding around the planet and into the
universe. I envision healing of humanity, Mother
Earth, and the differently sentient. May healing come
to you [name of person(s)]; and may healing come to
me… and I bow to the holy."*

I then close my morning prayer by giving thanks to
the universe; I reflect on all that I am grateful for, and
I stand. My mind is at peace and clear, and I begin
my day with an open heart of love. My prayer, even
to this day, continues to evolve and reflect the Caritas
Processes as a way of belonging.

The sutras of *love* and *grace* come to mind as I reflect on my daily ritual. Through this ritual, I send *out* unconditional gratitude and blessing to the universe: this manifests my sutra of love. At the same time, I'm sending gratitude and blessings *inward*… I'm reminding myself to love and forgive… myself: this manifests my sutra of *grace*. It is not easy. It is a work in progress. And I know that when I don't focus to start my day, I personally become imbalanced. And as a result of my morning prayer ritual — as a result of *love* and *grace* — I am no longer closed off from the universe. *Love* and *grace* have stopped me from hurting.

Reverence — respect and caring for all

Upon completing my period of travel, I returned to academia.

I started teaching palliative care and reconnecting with new and former colleagues in Watson's Caring Science. I took a post-doctoral position, and I learned how to wrangle big data and intersect palliative care with data science. I continued my own work in self-discovery and self-awareness and made intentional effort to be more mindful. I completed my post-doc and began working as an assistant professor at the College of Nursing.

Now, as a teacher (and life-long master learner), I integrate elements of an emancipatory caring relational pedagogy (Hills et al., 2020) in my practice. I model caring leadership and create an environment where students engage in equal learning with a shared vision — a communitas (I begin each class session with a centering exercise; I encourage open communication and one-on-one coaching sessions; I solicit feedback; I take time to reflect. I try to emulate what Jean did with me and my colleagues during our doctoral studies and create collaborative caring relationships). I recognize I am in a position of authority, but I am not authoritarian. And so now, I provide intentional space to respect and care for all those I encounter in my day-to-day life. This is my sutra of *reverence*.

Coda — the sutra as context-dependent, temporal, living entity

In my worldview, these sutras resonate with me from a caring ethic, an ethic I've long held. But it is only in recent months that I've taken time to name my emerging sacred sutras. I do not believe the sutras are static; they flow and shift like water as I change/evolve/learn within the infinitely changing/evolving/learning universe.

Even as I write my sacred sutras, I feel a calmness within myself. Like the sutras, I am defined and also ever-evolving — my definition is always changing, growing. The sutras and I mirror each other, help each other, and live together. In many ways, they've always been there. I just uncover them periodically, and in that uncovering moment, I treasure them as both fresh and eternal. Yes, the sutras are simple, elegant, and complete in explanation/translation — but also they are temporally bound, and they may be rendered incomplete by the future, which will yield the opportunity for me to "uncover" a new, perfectly complete (for that moment and that moment's version of me) sutra.

In short, the sutra is a way of being and becoming. As such, it is just like me — and just like you — and just like every living thing. The sutra is as it has always been: both a guide and a partner at every moment of this grand journey.

Sean M. Reed

PhD, APRN, ACNS-BC, ACHPN, AHN-BC, FCNS, SGAHN

Assistant Professor, University of Colorado, College of Nursing
Colorado

Sean is a first-generation college graduate from the Midwest who has been living in Colorado for over three decades. A multipotentialite with a diverse background and extensive experience, Sean has worked in numerous industries and roles, including entrepreneurship, hairdressing (despite being color-blind, he specialized in color), banking, business, and informatics. His colleagues and friends recognize him as a compassionate innovator, decisive leader, and imaginative out-of-the-box thinker.

Furthermore, Sean has a rich healthcare-focused background, having worked in massage therapy, ICU nursing, hospice, home care, palliative care, administration, research, and academic education. He serves as an active member of nursing organizations such as the National Association of Clinical Nurse Specialists and the Global

Academy of Holistic Nursing.

Sean is happily married to his husband Andrei, a Romanian citizen, for five years. Together, they share a passion for traveling around the world and immersing themselves in different cultural and spiritual traditions. Sean's exceptional life journey showcases his passion for his profession, his dedication to the Discipline, his openness to learning, and his appreciation for diversity.

Karen White-Trevino

Light

How I arrived at my personal sutra is a journey
of awakening. Approximately twenty years ago, the
word sutra was introduced to me by different yoga
instructors as I integrated poses and stretches to limit
physical injury. At that time, my understanding of the
word sutra was limited. Through the years, my yoga
practice became an important way to connect my
mind and body. Now, I am 60 plus years old, and this
manner of stoking my senses and fueling a lightness
in my physical body begins when I step on a yoga
mat. The mat is my place of solace as I calm the mind
and add poses (asanas) that challenge my aging body.
In addition, I have since explored this word, sutra.

I learned of Patanjali's sutras and specific practices
for a spiritual yoga journey while completing a yoga
teacher training program in Kauai, Hawaii. During
the six-month program, I was awakened to a deep
appreciation for the expansive meaning of this word

and other Sanskrit terms. Learning this ancient tradition fueled my intention to expand my mind-body connection to consciously include my spirit and soul. There was alignment with my Christian faith and beliefs and the yoga sutras. These parallel ways of being and belonging remain an important part of who I am. While developing a better understanding of sutra, my journey of awakening became a form of sacred service.

In this post-pandemic era, I listen to the words of Dr. Watson as she describes her own personal awakening and the call to elevate our discipline. She describes nursing's role in sacred service, activism, and expounds on her Seven Sacred Sutras: Stillness, Silence, Solitude, Spirit, Simplicity, Sacred Service, and Surrender (Watson, 2021). I eagerly accept her open invitation to go deeper to explore the spiritual caring-healing consciousness of our maturing nursing discipline and ourselves. In addition, these seven sutras or threads, intertwine with my individual beliefs and values, propelling me even deeper into my responsibility to role model sacred service and activism for humanity. This is a welcome invitation to fuel my spirit of inquiry while reinforcing spiritual caring-healing consciousness with the sutras of these wisdom leaders.

I also reflect on this awakening by the nurse sage, Dr. Watson, and my mind vacillates like pages in a book turning back and forth. How did we get to this moment of here and now, to this point in time that we label *post-pandemic*? My belief is that we must first surrender to the interconnectedness between humanity and the environment before our maturing discipline can transition to a new paradigm. The pandemic interrupted the human-environment connection and the light of humanity dimmed with death, despair and pain. Mother Earth tried to get our attention but had to break down and cry — her tears forcing humanity to stop and take notice.

Like me, many collectively prayed to the heavens… praying for hope, healing, and caring. Father Sky wiped the tears of Mother Earth and rekindled the flame connecting our humanity with the environment. The heavens and sky are our spiritual bellows, projecting each blast of air, like each breath of life, inviting humanity to release the grip of fear and despair and shift to a new paradigm of universal love.

To shepherd the shift to universal love, I share my personal sutra, *light*. The sutra, *light*, can be a physical or metaphysical vehicle. How do you visualize your *light*? Maybe you imagine a flame, the sun, the stars, the heavens, or a spirit. When I pause in silent prayer or during periods of stillness, I visualize this *light*, my inner spirit being, as bright beams from the heavens penetrating each of us. Just as the sutra of great yogis and Watson resonate with who I am and who I am becoming, my visualization of this inner spirit-filled *light* is my manner of connecting my spirituality deep within my soul. I know the feeling of a dimming spirit-filled *light* due to grief and emotional pain but I also have come to know the warm feeling of the beautiful rays of *light*, which may emanate from me when I experience joy and love.

I offer to anyone reading this sutra an opportunity to visualize your inner *light* and invite this *light* to nurture and heal so that you and those around you feel your inner glow. Raise your head looking towards the vast sky and be bathed in the natural sunlight. Close your outer eyes and feel the warmth of this sunlight envelop you with love and healing natural power… pausing for this brief caring moment. Embracing this sutra, *light*, as time stands still and allows you to be present. Adjust your gaze inward at the *light* that is residing within you. In this moment of stillness, visualize your *light* without judgment and surrender to this vulnerability. Why? Because you are loved. The inner rays of *light* desire to be in cadence with the ebb and flow of your breath for the rolling tides of this breath is in synchrony with the beating heart. The ebb and flow, the beating heart, are dance partners with the inner *light* connecting them. Now, this inner dance occurs lovingly through the contours of your soul.

Look inward, is your *light* dimmed? Our delicate humanness may weep for warmth, love, and *light*. The soul can gather energy from the pursed lips which are ready to gently propel your warm breath to fuel the crippled spark of *light* inside. The spark of *light* is craving to glow again, to awaken, as the inner soul craves another dance. Open the portal to usher in and reignite each ray. The inner dance of breathe-light-beating heart is yearning to warm and heal the soul. You will glow again. Your radiating *light* will weave a pattern with others and co-create a human-environmental pathway towards sacred service and activism. *You* are the *light*. *We* are the *light*, and *our* connected *light* will permeate throughout humanity while cascading healing energy and universal love.

Karen White-Trevino

DNP, RN, NE-BC, Caritas Coach®, RYT-200

Hawai'i

Karen grew up in Massachusetts, raised children in Texas & Florida, and now lives with her husband in Kaua'i, Hawai'i. Through these travels, she has strengthened a deep appreciation for connecting mind-body-spirit using the healing power of nature. Although her approach has changed throughout the years as she navigated life events, she remains fueled by loving family and friends. A nurse with over 40 years of experience, she integrates mentoring strategies to creatively balance the art and science of nursing. Now she has expanded mentoring, a sacred service, to include specific Caritas practices to nurture loving-kindness. Her inner passion is to create a safe and welcoming environment and empower people with sustainable mind-body-spirit practices infused with nature and a Caritas heart.

Jennifer Drake

From Reflection Emerge My Sacred Sutras

I really wasn't familiar with sacred sutras, until reading Caring Science as Sacred Science New Revised Edition (Watson, 2021), and taking a few classes with Jean Watson. I started to wonder more about what sacred sutras could mean to me.

I began reflecting upon the experience and events from the past few years. What were my simple truths? What was helping and guiding me? I couldn't name them before, now upon reflection they emerge as sacred sutras.

Gratitude

Gratitude was the first Sutra that came to mind. For years, gratitude was just saying thank you and being thankful, but I have learned that gratitude is so much more. Gratitude to me is like dropping a coin in a piggybank. Expressing gratitude fed my resilience and fostered connections with friends, family, and colleagues. It was those connections that helped me during the early days of the pandemic.

In the spring of 2020, the news was filled with terrifying information about a new virus, COVID-19, spreading across the country. I worked at a community hospital, and each day, we discussed plans for something we had never experienced. We were holding our breath. Then the pandemic came to our door and busted in. I remember a friend working in the emergency department texting, "Oh my god, we just tubed five patients. Where did they all come from?" When looking at our hospital census, another friend said, "They are on every unit. They are everywhere." Patients so very sick with COVID. I remember a nurse, in full personal protective equipment (PPE), standing with folded hands outside a patient's room, praying before she entered. Fear was surrounding and enveloping us all. I needed something to help me breathe. I turned to gratitude.

I have been blessed with friends of like minds. We were all seeking our own way at that time. Gathering courage each day to return. With one of my friends, at the beginning of my day, I would exchange messages of gratitude or photos of the angel pin I wore. She would send a picture of the televised daily Mass she was attending and a heart, letting me know she was praying for me, for all of us. This simple moment of connection was my first moment of gratitude each day. I took it in and found my courage to keep moving.

Gratitude today feels different. The practice from 2020 has grown to be my foundation for every day. No matter what is happening, I am so very grateful.

Grace

My lessons from gratitude lead me to *grace*. Grace for me is that inner feeling, that I am enough, that even if I don't finish everything at work, or if I can't always be physically present, I want to be and I am not failing! I am enough because of grace. It is an acceptance, deep down, that supports my emotional well-being and authentic self.

I seek to give myself grace when I stumble and cannot live up to the expectations of myself, and I offer grace to others who may not have met my expectations. Grace enables me to offer love and kindness and gratitude. I cannot imagine gratitude, without grace.

When I think of grace, I calm the voices of insecurity and inadequacy that call to me to ask me to give up. Grace reminds me to keep trying and recognize mistakes or missteps; reframing to help me and to not stop me. I continue to grow in grace, offering grace to myself and those around me. Grace has helped me with connections where before I would have run, seeking more comfortable relationships. Grace helps me grow.

Serenity

Serenity to me represents stillness, and within there, contentment. Serenity points me to something greater. I am learning that serenity and stillness bring peace and fill me more than anything. Silence used to stress me or worry me, as if silence were a void needing to be filled. However, silence is filled with compassion that we only need to reach in and scoop some out.

As a clinical educator, I'd often ask the room a question and the silence would feel so uncomfortable. I became impatient! I needed an immediate response to fill that silence. Fill that awkward uncomfortable space. However, now, I know grace helps me to pause and lean into the silence, seeking that serenity, that feeling that this moment is okay. Not to rush or demand a response or action.

Serenity has spread to so many other areas. I have this inner drive to always be productive. There is no time to be lost. I must be doing something! Remembering serenity, that peaceful stillness, reminds me it's okay, to just be present. A recent trip to Scotland reminded me of the importance of serenity. There was so much to do! I wanted to see everything, and go everywhere, but if I moved fast, I would not experience this place with serenity, I would miss so much. I found serenity in sitting on a bench, watching children running through the courtyard of a castle. I found great joy talking and feeding ducks who waddled to my table in a garden; I filled my lungs with cool crisp air and experienced silence sitting on a rock on the edge of the Atlantic Ocean. Seeking serenity calms my busy mind. It allows my soul to be present and releases the unnecessary guilt of being unproductive. On the contrary, stillness and serenity are very productive.

Tribe

I first thought of community, but *tribe* is more than community. Community can be those who are like-minded and those who are not. Community could be a mix of thoughts and beliefs. To me, tribe is a little tighter. Surrounding yourself with those who are of like minds and hearts. Those who are open to new thoughts and beliefs and feelings, and yet still embrace each other.

A sutra is a point toward something greater. I think of all the communities, families surrounding me. Our work family, a dance family, a fencing family, a Caritas family, and even more! We have so many communities and families that are knitted together because of like-mindedness. There is so much for me to learn from those who do not think like me, and I enjoy hearing their perspective. However, there is a comfort that I embrace that comes from belonging. The sense of belonging in my tribe. There is something about community that feels so much more important than before the COVID-19 pandemic.

I have done some reading of late. Sometimes for escapism and sometimes to find direction. I have read a lot of Brené Brown, and even learned how to find and listen to podcasts (yes, I know, it's not so hard, but it was new to me). I love how Brené Brown talks about vulnerability and connection. My last three sutras are linked to what I have learned from her books and her podcasts.

Awkward

There are more times than I can count when I have felt awkward. New experiences, new people and unfounded fears and insecurities trigger the awkward. Talking with loving kindness may at times feel awkward if we have not expressed those thoughts and feelings. I was once told that we cannot use the words "reflective of caring" because we cannot expect nurses to know what we are talking about. I asked, "Why not?" Why are we not allowed to express heartfelt love to another? I try to overcome my awkwardness and do it anyway. I don't always overcome the feeling, but I am at least trying, and I am beginning to be comfortable in the awkwardness.

Brave

One area in my life that I need to improve is bravery. I would like to be brave and daring, even if it feels a little scary or awkward. I must be brave. I have to keep trying. I was asked in a healing circle once, "What is my purpose?" There was a long time when I was unsure what my professional purpose was, but I am slowly finding it. I feel that to seek my purpose, I must be brave. I have to try.

Recent experiences have required me to be brave. New experiences, new losses, and new opportunities have all asked me to be brave. Each one, a different kind of bravery, but all still asking me, requiring me to find that inner courage and be brave. And yet, I have found strength and serenity when I step into my brave space.

Kind

There are so many ways to be kind. Presence is not needed, only intentionality and sincerity. To be kind, we need empathy and connection, human to human connection. We can always succeed if we are kind. Intentional kindness, every day. Expressing kindness and gratitude. Nothing is more important.

So, there they are. My personal sacred sutras. I have come back to this space over and over to see if I have changed my mind, and I haven't. I now have a big sticky note on my desk with my sacred sutras as a reminder. I keep seeking to move to that greater thing and whatever emerges for me will lead me to my next adventure, my next experience.

Jennifer Drake

DNP, RN, NPD-BC, ONC, Caritas Coach®, Caritas Leader™

Clinical Educator for Onboarding
Virginia

Jennifer is a Clinical Nurse Educator of 36 years of experience in nursing, the last 20 years in academia and professional development. She cares for the nurses, who care for the patients, with a specific interest in the new graduate nurse. At home, she enjoys sewing tiny pieces of fabric into quilts and then wrapping her family in her quilts she made with love. Traveling with her family is another passion. She takes pleasure in going on adventures especially to national parks and Disney World! When not on an adventure or sewing, you may find Jennifer at home taking pictures of her dogs sleeping or just being cute.

Debby Flickinger

The Alchemy of the H.E.A.R.T through
a Watson Caring Science Lens Harmony,
Enlightenment, Affirmation, Reflection,
Transcendence

> Listen now as Earth sheds her skin
> Listen as the generations move
> One against the other to make power
> We are bringing in a new story
> (Harjo, 2021, p.3)

It was early last year that I began to think about the heart and its knowing, deep connection to the earth as an alchemical process. I could hear the voices of feminine consciousness and the sacred feminine reaching deep into my heart and soul. Out of the blue, I was invited to present at a workshop in which I became acquainted with Daniel Deslauriers' (2020) heart-knowing in which he posits, "Something that exists beyond me and us, but that takes me — or us — to conceive of it" (p.11).

Using Dr. Allan Combs' (2009) definition, I define "[Feminine] Consciousness [as] the background, or simply the ground, of all [women's] experience" (p.3). Jean Bolen-Shinoda (2010) reminds us that it is "the return of the sacred feminine, the age of the daughter, is evolutionary; that is, it's part of the Human species' story." (p.23). She continues with "[t]he quality of wisdom we need [in this era] has to come from the feminine in both men and women" (p.23). I am strongly committed to the concept that to care for the earth and the world around one, one must care deeply for oneself in order to understand the deeper meanings of compassion, kindness, caring, trust, and inter-relational ways of being.

Before I go further, I wish to acknowledge Dr. Jean Watson for her continued support of my work. Overtime, she has become a mentor and friend. Our relationship is like a comfortable shoe as it fits like no other. I am deeply in awe of her, and I am in gratitude for her guidance. Watson's Caring Science continues to inspire me, keeps me going, and lays the foundation for all my work and its interconnections with all of humankind and with the natural world.

The Sutra of Making a Cake: What is an Alchemical Process?

Let's explore the concept of alchemy, as it might be told as a sutra or thread to begin the connections to H.E.A.R.T. The Merriam-Webster Dictionary (2022) defines alchemy as "an inexplicable or mysterious transmuting." For me, alchemy begins when I reach for a bowl filled with nothing more than the creative possibility of transformation. I swirl around my own ingredients, such as cake mix, eggs, and water. As I mix them together, they transform from their lumpy shape into a silky, creamy liquid. Once poured into the pan, and baked in the oven, it becomes food worthy of the gods. With the first bite, what emerges is a sense of heart, and I am transformed.

Syma Allard (2020) states:

"Of the three works, the yoga sutras have been especially influential on modern culture (para.16). "Yoga" is a Sanskrit word meaning to yoke or to unite. A yoke, or wooden beam, used between a pair of animals to allow them to pull a cart together, generally serves two functions: to unite the animals to said cart, and to control the movements of the animals using ropes attached to the yoke (para.17). Just as a yoke is a mechanism of control and unity, yogic practice is a mechanism of controlling the body, breath, senses and mind to enable more effective meditation for the purpose of liberation" (para.18).

As in making a cake, it is the egg yolk that connects the elements. In this case the yolks, just as the yokes in a yogic practice, serve to unite the mixture as a sutra and an alchemical process, liberating the ingredients to become one, and blend together in perfect harmony, but inevitably, in making a cake, one must be prepared for the element of surprise. Watson (2018), reminds us to be "Open to mystery and allow miracles to enter" (p.140). Perhaps the alchemical process of heart knowing is something we experience every day as we engage in this dance we call life, seeking transcendence with every step.

Furthermore, with each step we create a sutra or thread which weaves our connection with the universe. Heart knowing in itself becomes the yoke that binds together the following sutras. Before we continue, remember that I am using an acronym for H.E.A.R.T: **H**armony; **E**nlightenment: **A**ffirmation; **R**eflection: **T**ranscendence.

The Alchemical Process of Harmony

"You cannot just be by yourself alone; you have to inter-be with every other thing"
(Hanh, 2017, p. 28).

I have a recurring dream I call *Hope*. I live in a community that is thriving and stable; in the dream the community is in harmony with the land. People use the land mindfully and everything is thriving. More importantly, education has prepared idealistic leaders to strengthen a democracy with new ideas, vigor, and commitment.

Jeremy Taylor (1983) stated, "Dreams have long been associated with creative inspiration in the expressive arts, and this popular association has tended to obscure the equally dramatic and consistent history of dream-inspired scientific and technical discovery and innovation" (p. 6).

The words Caring Sustainability were like a wellspring, an alchemical process, that pushed up through my body like a geyser, to reshape and transform my doctoral work in sustainability. I realized that you cannot sustain anything without caring.

The harmony of caring and sustainability took me in a new direction. It became a new sutra or thread that brought me peace, joy, and wisdom at the same time. I realized that without harmony and balance life would be both chaotic and static. I was able to delve into the alchemical process of enlightenment.

The Alchemical Process of Enlightenment

> Maybe this one moment, with this one person,
> is the very reason we're here on Earth at this time.
> (Watson et al., 2005)

It was during my dissertation work that I had a cosmic "Aha" moment of enlightenment. I suddenly realized that Watson's work with her Caring Science and the Caritas Processes were interconnected with my work in Caring Sustainability. Caring Sustainability is a caring consciousness that reconnects self, others, and nature with the desired outcome of balance and harmony. I became aware of how we as a planet cannot survive without caring and love.

My dream, *Hope*, continues to bring me to the heart of my work, which is teaching Caring Sustainability, always remembering that Watson Caring Science is an alchemical process that reconnects self, others, and nature with a desired outcome of balance and harmony. As I see it, enlightenment comes from being able to see from a place of heart and caring. With enlightenment comes wholeness and eventually transcendence.

My colleague, Dr. Martha Brumbaugh Jacobsen (2006), shared the story of her 1992 vision quest. It provides an alchemical process of enlightenment as she merged with nature to gain a deep understanding of the nature of feminine consciousness in the wilderness:

"It's five-thirty AM. A crane just flew over my head. Oh! I survived! I did it! I am alive! Isn't life incredible? I just spent a night alone with no tent, no food, no fire, and I am alive! I survived a herd

of deer, a cougar, and humans. This is incredible!
I must go for a swim and thank the river. I must
thank the trees, the animals, and I must thank
myself!

I have learned that I can spend the night in the
woods and survive! I have learned that life is not so
serious! It's FUN! I have learned that distractions,
be they human, four-legged, fish, birds, reptiles,
or bugs, do not prevent people from finding
themselves. Only our perceptions do that. We are
what we perceive. Life is what we perceive it to be.
I have learned that the human body is not ugly. It's
true and natural form cannot be dictated by some
fashion magazine. We are all different, and we are
all beautiful.

Isn't life incredible? Now I must journey back to
camp. I can't wait to share my life with the other
women. Goddess! I am so happy to be a part of a
larger feminine consciousness.

"I am Firewalker, and I am alive!" (pp. 179-180)

As a sutra, Martha's experience with enlightenment
might be summed up in this way: The mother sat
inside a circle of stone to listen for the voices of spirit
and nature. She listened to the river, to the wind,

and the birds. When the first human arrived, she was patient, even though the intruder crossed the boundary of the circle to offer up a sweet-smelling flower. When two naked, noisy men arrived at the river to swim, she listened to their stories, and learned from them. Enlightenment came as an unexpected gift from not only the elements of the animals, and the birds, but from the humans she had been trying to avoid. Everything was good.

It is from the experience of enlightenment that the affirmations can emerge in a swirl of joy from the container in which alchemy happens.

The Alchemical Process of Affirmation

The Caritas Processes are, in a sense, an affirmation to wholeness. They provide us, as Dr. Watson said, "a language to communicate caring moments" (Watson, 2015, sec. 4.08). For the purposes of my work, I have interpreted Dr. Watson's Caritas Processes to be representative of how I walk in my life.

I have a deep appreciation for Watson's Caring Science and the Caritas Processes and use them as a guiding light in my life. For me, they act as insights into the everyday alchemy in our lives. I also acknowledge that caring and heart knowing bring us into a higher state of feminine consciousness and closer to the sacred feminine.

Here, I use five affirmations, modeled on Dr. Watson's (2008) work, to weave together an alchemical process to create a sutra of affirmation:

1. Trust the process and remain authentic to self and show up for others as a caring consciousness.
2. Be fully present in the moment, recognizing the deep belief in self and others.
3. Meet communities where they are: Caring Sustainability engages in sincere teaching-learning experiences that ascend from an appreciation of interconnectedness.
4. Create an ethereal space where beauty, comfort, dignity, and peace are facilitated.
5. The heart, soul, mind, and life source of self are elevated when we care for others.

As I walk in my garden, I am aware of the connectedness of all life. I see the soil, the plants, the rocks, the sky and the sun as threads or sutras that lead to heart knowing. This knowledge inspires me to create affirmations, and moreover, I can reflect on the many blessings in my life.

The Alchemical Process of Reflection

To illustrate reflection as an alchemical process, I will draw from the experience of writing this chapter, and the acronym H.E.A.R.T. I will also draw on heart knowing, Caring Sustainability, and nature. The idea is that when we reflect on our lives, we don't need to draw from the past, but we can stay in the moment, and call on our immediate experiences to afford us the opportunity to move in new directions.

The alchemical process of reflection allows us to be fully present, without blame or judgment, in the moment and to recognize a deep belief in self and others (Arrien, 1993). You inevitably have the opportunity to witness a sense of alchemy as you engage in questions, conversations, and dialog if you allow mystery to enter in and remain open to possibility.

When I write, I sit in front of my computer, with my books, photographs, and even my old Suzy Smart doll as a permanent altar. I close my eyes and take several deep breaths. It is a moment to clear my head and prepare myself to become a writer. For this chapter, I considered harmony, enlightenment, affirmation, and now reflection. Before I am done, I will also have approached transcendence.

As I looked at harmony, I was immediately connected to the thought of balance, caring, and the need to have respect for all living things. My doctoral work seemed to be the thread that connected me to heart knowing and the acronym H.E.A.R.T. More recently, my desire to connect my work to feminine consciousness, and the sacred feminine, has brought me closer to the importance of harmony in all we think, all we say, and all we do.

Martha's vision quest story brought me face-to-face with the enlightenment that can come from spending a dark night, alone on a riverbank. When she awakened and realized that she was still alive, her entire perception changed. The enlightenment that came in those few seconds after awakening changed her life forever.

Affirmations are crucial to the sutra of heart knowing. As a practice they guide us through all the other elements. It is affirmation that binds them together in the process of alchemy. The more we repeat them, the more power they hold, and the stronger our heart knowing becomes, and even stronger is the connection to the sacred feminine and feminine consciousness.

In reflection, I am reminded of something I considered a few years ago when I was considering developing an afterschool program for middle-school students. Our children are our promise for a brighter future for generations to come. If children can learn to create small rituals for healing, the garden can be an ideal setting for reflection and later, transcendence.

The Alchemical Process of Transcendence

The alchemical process of transcendence is the ability to truly hear from the heart. It is the final piece of HEART knowing. Alchemy allows miracles to happen as you embody heart, enlightenment, affirmation, and reflective processes.

Transcendence is the gold: It is what Jean Watson (2015) refers to as the doing. Perhaps, alchemy is something we experience every day as we engage in this dance we call life, seeking transformation with every step. For me, the alchemy began when I stepped into a container filled with the creativity of heart knowing. I was swirled around with my own worldview; one of feminine consciousness and into the sacred feminine. What emerged was a sense of HEART. I was walking a path to transcendence.

In Closing

I leave you with a centering exercise that I do that focuses on this chapter.

- I breathe out chaos and disparity.
- I, slowly, breathe in harmony, enlightenment, and affirmation.
- I breathe out contradiction and turmoil.
- Slowly, I breathe in the desire for reflection and transcendence.
- I breathe out anything that is holding me back from the willingness to embrace heart knowing.
- I, slowly, breathe out the heart of alchemy.

I hope that this chapter has inspired you and will help

you to see your own alchemical processes as sutras for creating and embracing endless possibilities.

Debby Flickinger

PhD, Caritas Coach®, and Eco-Therapist

Affiliated Faculty, Ph.D. Enrollment and Engagement Specialist at Union Institute University California

Debby Flickinger, PhD, is an affiliated faculty at Union Institute and University (UIU) teaching doctoral courses on social justice, engaging differences, and sustainability through a caring science lens. She facilitates workshops, participates in panels, and does presentations on Caring Sustainability, Caring Science Theory, Critical Race Theory, and Social Justice around the globe. Also, a PhD Enrollment and Engagement Specialist at UIU.

She has contributed a chapter in *Miracles and Mysteries Witnessed by Nurses*, (Lotus Library 2019) a collection of stories edited by Jean Watson, Ph.D. Dr. Flickinger has collaborated on a book chapter for a book, Innovative Strategic Planning and International Collaboration for the Mitigation for Global Crisis (edited by Gabriela Antošová) published in January 2022. In addition, she is certified as a Caritas Coach®, an Eco-therapist, and a Sustainability Coach.

She received her Ph.D. from the California Institute of Integral Studies in Transformative Studies with a concentration in Consciousness Studies, a MA in Consciousness and Transformative Studies, and BA in Philosophy and Religion from John F. Kennedy University.

Sutras

Lending

Practice

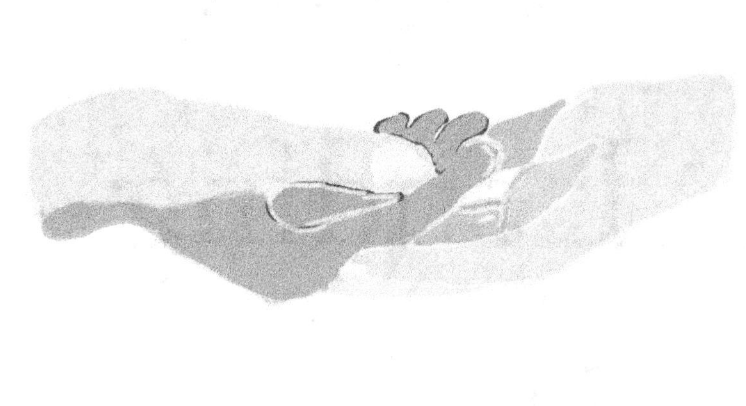

Danielle Leone-Sheehan

Sacred Sutras in the Intensive Care Unit

As a nurse practicing from the frame and philosophy of Watson's Caring Science, I have always resonated with the connection and orientation of the theory with the spiritual. I resonate most closely with the third Caritas Process, "Being sensitive to self and others by cultivating one's own spiritual practices — beyond ego to transpersonal presence" (Watson, 2018). The journey away from ego-orientation requires a connection and deeper knowing of spirit, a reaching toward that which is both greater than ourselves and also serves to connect all humanity. This connection to spirit is constantly needing to be renewed. My experience of Watson's Seven Sacred Sutras are as an opportunity and guide toward that deeper connection and continuous renewal of spirit.

I frame my experience of the sacred sutras in

my clinical work as a nurse in the intensive care unit (ICU). This work brings me in contact with patients and families in crisis, facing uncertainties and the possibility of death. In critical illness, we are pushed to explore meaning and purpose, and that which is greater than us. Not all nurses are prepared to face these challenging clinical situations as an opportunity for personal exploration, but it remains that each encounter opens a door to greater understanding of spirit and self.

Stillness

Stillness is an opportunity for renewal and to connect with the bigger picture. As I rush from task to task, work through new orders, more labs, ringing phones, a growing checklist, I take the opportunity to stop and wait. I may be waiting for a lab result, waiting for a medication to be delivered. This waiting may be just a minute, but in that waiting, that stillness, I don't seek to do anything but just to stop and be. In my own stillness I am able to, in the midst of all the busyness, connect with that which is beyond the checklist, connect more fully with that which is greater. Greater purpose, greater understanding, greater connection to the patient and family receiving my care. In stillness, we step beyond the constant doing and connect with what it means to just be.

A story of Stillness

He came to us confused, not responding. He hadn't eaten in several days. Losing his connection with the outside world, his purpose, his independence. His loss had been progressive over the last few years but made worse by this current illness. He hardly heard me, hardly responded, receiving care as if a bystander to his own circumstances. I was busy and heavily clothed in the protective equipment needed to care for him. Rushing in and out, drawing labs, hanging medications, completing procedures to support his body. One medication a few drips away from done, another waiting to be hung, I still myself and wait. In this waiting, I had nothing to do, no task left to complete. I knew if I stepped out of the room, I would need to come right back in a matter of minutes to hang the next medication. So, I waited. I stood in stillness and something miraculous happened, I saw him, the whole him. I saw the whole life that had brought him to that moment and the troubled life that lay ahead. In my stillness I saw him and connected with him and cared for him, body, and spirit.

Silence

Hospitals are places seldom described as silent. Even in the middle of the night, there are alarms, phone calls, patients arriving at the emergency department and requiring immediate care. This is particularly true of my work in the ICU. Despite this, I connect with the sutra silence in many ways.

A story of Silence

She was so tired. Newly diagnosed with her illness, she was physically tired from having not slept and emotionally so under the weight of what was to come. I cared for her in the night. I was in and out of the room, hourly, more than hourly, frequently checking labs, giving medications. I slipped in and out, the room dark and the door closed behind me. And through my silence she slept. Even with the frequent prick of a finger, she

half opened her eyes to see me and drifted back
to sleep. In our shared silence, we were connected.
She trusted me as I became part of her room,
part of her subconscious, slipping in and out as
she slept. So tired, protected by her trust in me,
protected by the silence.

Solitude

As a teacher, a nurse, and a mother of small
children, I am rarely alone. In constantly being with
and giving to others, it is easy to lose myself. I find
that I crave and search for those moments of solitude,
however fleeting. I find them often at the ends. The
end of the day, after all have drifted off to sleep in
my home. The end of a shift, as I embark on my
long drive home. In this solitude, I can more fully
see myself, my values, my beliefs, my faith. It opens
a window into my soul and allows me to reconnect
with my purpose.

A story of Solitude

The family had gone and what remained was her

body. All the pumps had stopped, the ventilator was silent, and the dialysis disconnected. The monitor turned off as the heart had completed its last beat allowing her soul to be free. What remained was her body and me. In my solitude I cleaned removing lines and tubes, taking down drips, washing her body. In my solitude I saw myself, my own life, my own beating heart, my own soul, my own death. I cared for her body as if my own and in that solitude, I found peace.

Spirit

I have often felt the most connected to spirit, not in the seeking, but in the letting go. In the invitation to possibility, in the trust in that which is wiser and greater than myself, it is then that I am truly connected with spirit. Despite this as a nurse in the ICU, I often seek to control. I control my patient's vital functions with medications and interventions. I serve as a gatekeeper for their care, controlling when visitors may enter, when tests may be completed. Within my control, I anticipate what will come next, I anticipate if they will become better or worse leaving nothing up to chance. As an experienced nurse, I have learned to let go of this perception of control. We are never completely in control, we can never fully anticipate how our patient's illness will progress, we make our best guess, and follow our best course. In accepting my lack of control, something unexpected happened in my care. In letting go, I created an opening for hope, an opening for miracles, and an opening for spirit.

A story of Spirit

I had cared for her for weeks. Her brain wracked by seizures we were unable to control, disease that had spread beyond our best treatments. There was talk of damage unrepairable, no return of function, no hope. I cared for her body. I spoke with her, expecting no response, asking her to squeeze my hand, open her eyes. I provided updates to her husband. I saw her through his eyes. I saw the love he had for her, the hope he had that she would come back to him whole, recovered, the women he had fallen in love with. I opened myself to his hope, despite the reports from the neurologist. Night after night, I cared for her. Asking her to squeeze my hand, expecting no response, opening myself up to hope, to spirit, to that which is greater than myself. Then one night, I asked her to squeeze my hand and she did.

Simplicity

Care of patients in the ICU can be very complex. Patients have multiple diagnoses, numerous medications, complicated family dynamics. We, the care team, often get caught up in the details, caught up in the complexity, and miss the greater picture. Multiple services come in and out, treating just one part of the patient: wound care, cardiology, urology. In the center of this complexity is the patient and the nurse. Only here at the center can the whole be seen and the focus be understood.

A story of Simplicity

I was sitting at the desk charting. A young nurse emerged from her patient's room with a family member, a woman. The woman she was with was visibly upset. The young nurse was struggling to explain everything that was going on in the room, all the procedures, all the tests, what was working and what wasn't and why. The woman wasn't satisfied, she didn't understand. She pushed the young nurse further. The nurse stepped back in the room telling the woman that she needed to care for her loved one. I stood up from my seat and walked over to the woman. I asked her how she was, I asked her to tell me about her loved one, I asked her how we could help her through this time. I didn't speak with her about tests, or procedures, or medications. I focused on the simple center in the middle of this complex care, the patient, the person that she loved, and her own pain. The woman thanked me, no longer focusing on the complexity and instead on her loved one as she felt more secure and connected and less lost. The young nurse emerged from her room, apprehensive to speak again with the woman. The woman told her she was going home and thanked her for her care.

Service

What drew me to nursing in the first place was a call to service. I wanted to help others in whatever way I could; and nursing gave me an opportunity to do so. In choosing to work as a nurse in the ICU, I sought to serve the most critically ill patients who required the most complete care and service. I also serve my profession as a nurse educator, working to develop the next generation of nurses, helping to prepare them to step into service of the profession. A call to service is one of humility, where we humbly are called to use our gifts to serve others. In my professional work, I am not seeking to be honored and glorified, but to humbly use my gifts in service of others. It is in the connection to service that I am able to see the true purpose of my work.

A story of Service

I entered nursing with the intent to serve, without fully understanding what that meant. As a high-achieving student, I saw potential in my hands, potential to heal and potential to save. While in clinical in long-term care, I met a nurse who had been working on the same floor for decades. She worked in service to her residents and out of love for them. I lacked appreciation/ respect for the work she was doing, thinking it not complex/skilled. One night toward the end of our clinical rotation, she told me that the hands of a nurse were acting in the service of God. Her words touched me in a way that I couldn't have expected. I looked then to my own hands. In judging this nurse's work in long-term care, I had lost sight of the true meaning of service. The words of that nurse helped me to let go of the notion that I would save, that I would heal, and instead allowed me to begin my nursing career with humility in service of my patients and in service of God.

Surrender

The seventh sacred sutra, surrender, feels the most personal to me. For me surrender is interconnected with spirit. I surrender my perception of control with a knowing that I never truly had that control in the first place. Something greater is carrying me when the unexpected occurs and I take comfort in that. Not only comfort but deeper connection and alignment with that which is greater.

A story of Surrender

She lay quietly in the bed, surrounded by lines,

tubes, and machines supporting her body. Care decisions had been made consistent with her values, her wishes, her beliefs. Her husband then said, "Now it's in God's hands." We, the care team, step out of the room. The resident physician labels them "religious" in a way that is not at all flattering. The respiratory therapist calls them "delusional." I call them, "accepting." They have accepted that whatever happens next is out of their control. They have accepted where they are at this current moment. They have surrendered themselves to what will come. They are brave and at peace.

Danielle Leone-Sheehan

PhD, RN, Caritas Coach®

Assistant Professor, School of Nursing and
Health Sciences, Merrimack College
Clinical Nurse,
Beth Israel Deaconess Medical Center
New Hampshire

Danielle is an Assistant Professor of Nursing at Merrimack College, in North Andover MA. Danielle also works as a registered nurse in an Adult Intensive Care Unit at Beth Israel Deaconess Medical Center, in Boston MA. Danielle's practice and research interests are grounded in Watson's Caring Science. Danielle serves on the Massachusetts Regional Caring Science Consortium Executive Leadership team and is a board member for the International Association for Human Caring. In addition to her work, she enjoys spending time with her family and reading, exploring, and laughing with her children, Frankie and Rachel.

Gloria Littlemouse

Thank You, Great Spirit

I open my eyes
Roll to my back
Put my feet on the floor
To give thanks

Got coffee in hand
With much to be done
Try drinking
With a mask

This shift will be long,
no charge nurse today
My patient is trying,
to get out of bed

Help me, Great Spirit
Get to the end of my day

My moccasins are worn
My back is sore

I've never had to work
So hard before
The sub variants are here
And numbers are rising
I need to go outside
And breathe in silence

It's all about me
In order to help others
I must enter in peace
To give some sense of relief

Who cares about me
It's so hard to see
This bloody disease
Took the best of me

I Love what I do
Or should I say it past tense
Because no one understands
Mindfulness

Take a deep breath in
And breathe out slow
I'll go to bed now
Until it's time to go

Gloria Littlemouse

PhD, RN, Caritas Coach®, HTP, EOL Doula

Watson Caring Science Postdoctoral Scholar
Mother Earth

Dr. Gloria Littlemouse (Diné) is a current postdoctoral fellow under the guidance of Living Legend Dr. Jean Watson and the Watson Caring Science Institute. Dr. Littlemouse is a seasoned healthcare professional with over three decades of experience in ICU nursing, hospice care, and academia, She is committed to promoting and implementing Caritas Processes One by teaching healthcare professionals to Practice Loving Kindness in all healthcare settings. Working during COVID for her was traumatic and now it is time for all nurses to heal, one hug at a time. Dr. Littlemouse is currently working on Self-Care research to help heal the profession and inspire a new generation of caregivers who are committed to promoting a culture of compassion and kindness with priority on self-care. Better self-care will give us resilience to handle the storms. Every next generation of nurses are the future and we must ensure they have the tools to keep them healthy and supported with Love and

Kindness to create a brighter future for all, just like the beautiful humming bird who flutters and spreads love to all the young buds. Life is short, share LOVE and feed a hummingbird.

Julie Piazza

Poems of Sutras

Changes

Witnessing nature unfolding
Life emerging
Embracing challenges
At every turn
Living in the moments
Drinking it all in
Gulping
Will there be enough of me?
Saying farewell
To memories, people, things
Painful and joyful
At the same time
You know the plans, Lord
Future and hope
Banking on that promise
Hoping for healing
Grateful for what has been healed
Just around the river bend…

Help me wait
And discover with guidance
The tools and the opportunities
To cope, comfort, and sustain
In these new waters
Changes ahead

June, 2020

Provisions and Presence

I am so blessed
The cup is overflowing
My heart is singing with joy
The days fly by
And we learn more about ourselves and one another
Bless us and keep us
Guide and protect us
Instill within us
The hunger to explore
Our deepest fears
And our greatest joys
Humble curiosity leads the way
Synergy fuels our hearts
The hedge of protection
Allows for openings to peek
Onto our path while
Remaining aware of
What is needed for the journey?
The wings and the groundedness
It will take to get us there with anointed
Provisions and presence

June 21, 2022

Creating a Healing Environment: The Elements of a Sutra Practice

Compassion begins with me
The power of a pause
The stillness
Intentions set
To thoughtfully consider and observe
What is before me, beside me, and behind me?
A full circle reflection
Supports and strengthens
The healing environment
And it begins with me

August 14, 2022

Julie Piazza

MS, CCLS

**Administrative Lead, Interprofessional Research
Committee, Senior Project Manager,
Office of Patient Experience, Michigan Medicine,
University of Michigan Health
Michigan**

Julie is a child life specialist, researcher, and project manager with the Office of Patient Experience at Michigan Medicine, University of Michigan Health. Julie's efforts are always to work towards partnerships with patients, families and interdisciplinary staff to improve the human experience through creating healing environments and building communities. A practicing artist, she loves to paint, photograph, create nature-based collages and sculptures and breathe in the world's beauty.

Her favorite things are innovation and compassionate lifelong learning along with her tender loving family who help her stay the course, explore, and discover the best things in life through privileged presence!

Sutras Lending Wisdom

Priscilla Javed

Sutra: Self-awakening…

journey to self

After recently retiring from my dream job, I entered a transitional time filled with freedom to define the next chapter of my life. I chose to welcome this quiet space and deeply reflect on my past, dream about the future, and engage in now moments. My home is filled with numerous books and several of them are unread. I started reading, seeking new knowledge from unfamiliar sources. Attending virtual and in-person courses on unfamiliar subjects became my new norm. As the days passed, I realized I was coming back home to my Heart and discovering new ways of Being. It was as if my spiritual, soulful self-woke up.

Within the literature, often enlightenment is synonymously aligned with awakening and realization. Most importantly, they imply there is a deeper-self within us that is our true conscious state of wholeness or oneness with Being, awaiting beyond the mind. Self-awakening is a personal journey of deepening the relationship with self. For me, it means connecting with my conscious state of 'Being', finding inner peace, walking awakened within in this world.

Inner Experiences toward Self-awakening

Self-questioning - reflective practices offer time to recenter and repattern how we want to devote our precious moments.

Start with asking yourself questions: Who am I? Why am I here? What was my purpose and is it my purpose now? How do I want to spend my time, moments? Allow for the emergence of your own thought-provoking questions to increase your whole self-awareness, mind, ego, body, and spirit. Use this time to reflect on external and internal influences that have contributed to your personal evolution. Engaging in this thought-provoking process offers an opening toward enlightenment, lighting your path for discovering your true-Being.

Inner listening - the majority of our daily communication is spent with ourselves, not others; learn to listen to internal conversations with intent of developing a relationship with self.

Pause and listen to your conversations. Are your thoughts putting you down? Judging others? Is your language motivating or suppressing? Are your thoughts invoking reactive behaviors? Our thoughts, feelings, emotions affect our demeanor along with health and wellbeing. Entering this self-listening practice offers a new portal for discovering self-embodiment, identifying fears, language, and behaviors that hinder our growth keeping us living in an unconscious state of mind. The continuous mindless chattering, the preoccupied ego, is not our true essence. Disengage from this energy draining incessant unconscious thinking activity. We are not just thinkers. When we become observers, aware of our emotions, thoughts, and responsive actions, we move into the realm of consciousness (Tolle, 2004).

Curious exploring – this self-learning journey invites the learner to deepen their worldly awareness by exploring desired learning experiences, the what, why, how from whoever's viewpoint.

Enrich thyself, start by sorting through your current books to identify the ones you haven't read but still want to read, or those you want to reread. If none of the books spark your curiosity, then what are you yearning to learn? Research the subject, find resources, articles and books, and begin reading, exploring new ways of knowing and doing. Connect with more authors found within the readings, be open to discovery, and welcome a new realm of learning that can ignite your passion and present growth possibilities toward being and becoming. Move forward through your fears, connect with others, embrace new avenues of learning by searching for intriguing courses, classes, conferences, programs, retreats, travel, organizations. Be free to nurture your authentic self.

Mindful Practicing – post the exploration phase, the journey to self-awakening calls upon us to change or initiate new learned practices.

Practice, practice, and more practice is vital for creating new heartfelt renewal rituals centered on finding inner peace. Select your new practices and begin doing what allows you to find the conscious state of Now, inner stillness, and shift away from the unconscious state of the ego mind. These could be yoga, meditation, poetry, photography, gardening, nature walks, just listen to your Heart. Choose approaches that assist you in becoming authentically present in the moment and finding your true essence of 'Being'. You are your own biogenic source to realize inner peace and find 'self' at a deeper level, trust yourself!

Intuitive Awakening - by engaging in these developmental experiences, new ways of knowing are illuminated allowing the emergence of inner peace, being in the moment.

This personal realization surfaces when we become aware that there is a deeper self beyond our thoughts, the unconscious state, and encounter living in the now, the conscious state. As we stimulate this higher level of consciousness, Tolle (2004) states "You also realize that all the things that truly matter – beauty, love, creativity, joy, inner peace – arise from beyond the mind. You begin to awaken" (p.17). From this awakened space, a sense of freedom yet belongingness with the world arose. I felt connected with others, a sense of vast 'oneness' unfolded. And realized, we have the potential to share our love and light universally to influence our world.

I am perfectly imperfect within this world,
Seeking the inner 'core' beauty in self, and others.
True self lies within this sacred realm
Like a seed longing to be nurtured.
Looking through the lens of Love

I unlock the mystery of One's wholeness.
Listen, be silent, be present, love thyself and others
Watch caring moments and miracles unfold.
Accept new ways of Being to find Inner Peace
Rejoice for becoming in Love with humanity.
Priscilla Javed

Reference

Tolle, E. (2004). *The Power of Now: A Guide to Spiritual Enlightenment*. New World Library and Namaste Publishing.

Priscilla Javed

DNP, RN, CENP, FACHE Caritas Coach®,
HeartMath Certified Trainer

WCSI Caring Science Postdoctoral
Scholar Faculty Associate,
Watson Caring Science Institute
Adjunct Faculty, University of San Francisco
California

Dr. Priscilla Javed is the Former Regional Director of Nursing Professional Practice in Northern California for Kaiser Permanente Patient Care Services and Nurse Scholar's Academy. Priscilla's responsibilities included program oversight and spread of Caring Science, HeartMath, Leadership Development, Nurse Executive Fellowships, and Advanced Degrees to elevate nursing professional practice. Priscilla's expertise as a Caritas Coach® and HeartMath trainer ensured programs were deliberately grounded in Caring Science, Heart-Centered methodologies.

Priscilla obtained her Doctor of Nursing Practice (DNP) with an emphasis in executive leadership from the University of San Francisco (USF) in 2016. Dr. Jean Watson's theory of

Human Caring and Transformational Leadership theorists guided her doctoral project titled 'Transforming Self and Systems through implementation of a Caring Coach Leader program'. This scholarly work influenced curriculum development for two leadership development succession planning pathways for nurse executive advancement and fellowships. Priscilla returned to USF in 2019 to start a new chapter of her life as Adjunct Faculty for the School of Nursing and Health Professions. Today, Priscilla continues to deepen her scholarly endeavors as a WCSI Caring Science Postdoctoral student by exploring new ideas to build upon currently published literature on quantum caring healthcare leadership principles.

Patricia Crispi

Finding Joy

It seems as if everyone is asking this question lately: "What brings you joy?" It was not until I listened to a presentation by a Caritas Coach® who provided a template to list ten things that bring the most joy that I truly paused and reflected on what encompasses my greatest joys. To begin, I needed a working definition for joy. Brown (2021), defines joy as "an intense feeling of deep spiritual connection, pleasure, and appreciation." This precise definition incorporates Watson's Seven Sacred Sutras perfectly: Stillness, Silence, Solitude, Spirit, Simplicity, Sacred Service and Surrender.

Family

Family is always the obvious response to the

question of what brings us joy. Of course, being surrounded by people you love is one of the greatest pleasures in life, but further reflection was needed to articulate precisely what about my family brings me the most joy. As I pondered this, I realized that it is being available and authentically present with my family as my fullest and best self that is truly joyful. The stillness of holding a sleeping baby or lovingly watching a sleeping teenager just before stirring them from sleep. The simplicity of a family game night or eating ice cream. Laughter. The meaningful solitude in acknowledging that I am the one and only mother to these amazing children. The husband who loves me enough to surrender into this incredibly fulfilling journey. The silence in a still house knowing that all are out doing what brings them the most joy and establishing without their knowledge how they live their own sacred sutras. The surrender to messy disarray when backpacks and sporting equipment are dropped carelessly and scattered like land mines about the family room. The spirit of laughter when the yard is full of friends splashing in the pool or playing competitive wiffle ball. This is *joy*.

Physical Activity

Physical activity is another "go to" when asked what brings me joy. My reflection revealed that it is not the accomplishment of the physical component of the activity, yet it is the wonder of the pink and golden sunrise that catches my breath as a morning comes alive. It is the opportunity to connect with loyal friends to discuss whatever topic comes to mind on routine morning runs. It is the wind in my face as I am cycling with my dedicated team as we train to ride in the name of sacred service to help those suffering from the chronic effects of multiple sclerosis. It is the way this team also makes me laugh as we tease each other endlessly and share in the spirit of camaraderie. It is the way my mind and body feel when any of these activities are complete; the simplicity of accomplishment, endorphins invigorating my soul, the way my body feels flexible, powerful, and strong.

Joy whispers in distinctive ways to different people yet it is a word that tends to be tossed around rather loosely. If one carefully considers joy through a thoughtful process while being authentically present with the intense feelings that come from joy, it is possible to savor in the moment and recognize that

no matter the challenges, there is joy to be found.
May you be blessed with joy in any form.

Patricia S. Crispi

PhD, RN, NPD-BC

Nurse Director, Patient Care Services, Quality, Safety, and Professional Development
Massachusetts

Patricia Crispi is the Nurse Director of Patient Care Services Quality, Safety, and Professional Development at Newton-Wellesley Hospital, which is part of a community division of hospitals within the Mass General Brigham system in Massachusetts. She earned her PhD in Nursing as part of Endicott College's graduating class of 2022 where she delivered the commencement address on behalf of the college's graduate students. Her dissertation research study is titled Exploring Relationships Between Health-Promoting Self-Care Behaviors Among Nurses and their Perceived Incidence of Presenteeism. Watson's Caring Science provided the theoretical framework for her research as she is passionate about unitary caring science and its importance in providing holistic, personal, and authentic nursing care.

Patricia lives in Norwood, MA with her husband Peter, daughter Megan and son Jamie who inspire her with love, meaning, and purpose in every aspect of daily life. Without their generous love and support, it would not be possible to continue the drive and passion to incorporate health-promoting self-care practices into the working environments for nurses and to provide the space where nurses can be authentically present with patients who have entrusted them to provide them the incredible of gift of care.

Natalya Yim

Surrender

*As we fall, and we are always falling, we can surrender
to the cause of falling.
We can relax our gates that hold our identities, our
nature, and our molecular structure,
And allow new connections, directions, and chemical
reactions to change our minds and body.
Falling is not a failure because it brings us to where we
can see the beauty of the moon,
Feel the breath of the earth, and dissolve into the
lightlessness of the universe.
We are like snowflakes falling from the sky and
carrying the messages of infinity, love, and compassion.
We can fall kicking and screaming hoping to disrupt the
order in which we are falling, but
We only disrupt our inner world and make ourselves
more vulnerable and resistant to change.
As we fall, we come into contact with other falling
people, subatomic particles, and ideas.
When we surrender our desires, failures, and goals, we*

become lighter and do not hit the ground prematurely. Surrender to the cause of falling and become suspended in the infinite field of emptiness and stillness.

Natalya Yim

MSN, MBA, RN

Staff Nurse, Cedars Sinai Medical Center
California

Natalya Yim is a staff nurse currently working in perioperative care at Cedars Sinai Medical Center, Los Angeles. As a critical care nurse, Ms. Yim has 15 years of experience working in acute care settings. She is experienced intensive care unit and emergency department nurse. In her present capacity, Ms. Yim works closely with patients undergoing joint replacement surgeries.

In May of 2021, Ms. Yim graduated from Grand Canyon University with a Master of Business Administration and Master of Nursing Science with emphasis on Nursing Leadership in Healthcare Systems. Currently, Ms. Yim is pursuing Doctor of Philosophy degree in General Psychology with emphasis on Industrial and Organizational Psychology from Grand Canyon University. She believes that nurses should be actively involved in healthcare management and reforms.

Her long-term professional goals include mentoring and supporting nursing leaders and bedside nurses who are instrumental intellectual forces in restoring the wellbeing and health of individual people, communities, countries, and populations.

Ms. Yim loves cooking and spending time with her two children, husband, and sister-in-law. Her son is a graduate student at the University of California, Davis and her daughter is a 4th grade elementary school student. Natalya and her children enjoy making origami and learning from nature.

Rita Romito-DiGiacomo

Finding Meaning in Watson's Sacred Sutras

The Wind is the Playground of Birds

The wind is the playground of birds,
Swirling gusts flowing under their feathered wings,
Lifting and gliding them along brisk and unseen paths,
With little energy needed or used, they fly joyfully.
Let us learn from the birds,
For rather than walking against the winds of life,
May we turn and let our wings catch the wind,
Riding and sailing the unseen paths,
Freeing us from worry or concern,
And finding joy in the flight.

Sacred Sutras and what they mean to me

For me, the sacred sutras are spiritual tools/ practices that help me to navigate my caring practice as well as my place in the universe. Just as our five senses guide our body, the sacred sutras guide my practice and help to strengthen my mind and spirit. Nature provides the perfect healing space to practice sacred sutras. When I think of nature, I see a gateway to Mother Earth's soul and to universal connectedness. We all share this one planet. We get to experience its beauty and life-sustaining forces, uniting us in love and harmony. It is the temple that allows me to practice and sustain the sacred sutras. I find peace, calm, and renewed energy just by sitting in stillness, breathing, feeling nature around me. Whether I am taking in the visual beauty, feeling the warmth of the sun, hearing the birds singing, or the gentle waves on a beach, nature always feels like a sacred and connecting space for me.

I can connect to nature and the sacred sutras by holding treasures that Mother Earth gives me, such as intricate shells, beautiful stones, or lovely flowers. Nature always impresses me; from its flowery fragrances, to the splendor of towering trees. By immersing myself in nature, I can escape to a place of peace, and it is there that I feel the most connected to all life forms and to our humanity, knowing that we are always sharing this sacred, life-sustaining planet.

Stillness

Stillness allows me to hold sacred universal space quietly and with an open heart, freeing my mind, body, and soul so that I can have a broader vision of my path and purpose. It fully reveals to me the beautiful tapestry we weave through our caring practice. By rooting myself to Mother Earth and her healing energy, I have a greater sense of our universal connectedness. It reminds me of how we are all grounded to this one sacred vessel, energies flowing together.

Silence

Silence allows me to surrender myself, stepping away from the noise of life, away from fear, stress, and worry. For me this is best done by stepping into a sacred space. My favorite sacred space is immersing myself in nature, where the only sounds I hear are trees swaying in the wind, birds singing sweet songs, the lullaby of crickets, and the sound of ocean waves. It is here that I can silence my mind and discover my purpose. It is here I can hear the universe calling to me, guiding me on my path; and through my sacred practice I can transfer this silence and stillness.

Solitude

Solitude allows me to draw from self to listen to the needs of my mind, body, and soul, and nurture them. I enter a space sealed from the rest of the world, either physically or in my mind's eye. A place of beauty, peace, security, and serenity, where anything is possible if you believe. A place where your mind is free to explore your sacred purpose, to think beyond earthly possibilities, and to know that universal connections are always at work, guiding us to our next path and purpose.

Spirit

For me, caring for another human being is a sacred practice, one which connects our spirit to those we care for. As we allow our spirit to make that connection, we help to balance them when they are unbalanced by illness. We can bring hope, understanding, and healing. We can help to guide them on their journey to recovery, or we can help to transition them to the spiritual world. We can connect our heart energy with the heart energy of our patients, utilizing its loving energy, compassion, and harmony, as well as our healing presence to comfort, guide, and hold our patients with unconditional love, transferring healing and sustaining energy.

As a Catholic, spirit represents my faith and loving connection to God. It is a gateway to the Father, who is always guiding me on my earthly journeys. I believe that people of all faiths can connect through the shared gateway of universal love and prayer, letting spirit be the compass to our practice.

Simplicity

For me, simplicity is to pare down, to stay on the surface rather than attempting to find light in dark waters. Sometimes our practice sends us down complicated, multifaceted paths attempting to control what we cannot control, twisted paths of "what if," or "if only." By simplifying, we trust in our path, we trust in our abilities, and above all, we trust in our faith and the greater universal plan. In nature, I can practice this sacred sutra by reflecting and appreciating how all life forms live in harmony with one another, how balance is peacefully maintained. I believe that is truly freeing to witness and draw from.

Service

Our sacred service to others allows us, as caregivers, to be a mediator of universal connections. We can bring together our shared experiences, which promotes hope and healing. For example, by sharing past sufferings, whether they are personal experiences or witnessed through a loved one, we can help patients who are currently on a similar journey. By guiding and comforting those experiencing similar pain, we can form this special spiritual and healing connection through our shared suffering, holding and guiding them, and even healing ourselves through this sacred and holy connection. I have had so many of these experiences calling back the pain, suffering, and uncertainty of why this is happening to a loved one and years may go by until the universe connects me to another person on a similar journey. My experience helps me guide them, encourage them, and give them strength and hope on their journey, which in turn helps me to find purpose and peace in my own suffering.

In nature, I can reflect on my service to others, as well as give my service to Mother Earth; to care for her and do what I can to help protect and sustain her and all the life forms she holds. Mother Earth is our universal life force, a sacred vessel that holds our humanity, our sacred service to one another, and our spiritual practices, cradling us all lovingly and equally.

Surrender

Surrender represents releasing the hold that perceived control can have on us. It is a grip that can drain us of vital energy and hope that we need in our sacred practices. By surrendering, we can trust and believe in divine and universal purpose, that all is as it should be. It is important to trust in unseen paths, and in our intuition. We must understand that suffering is part of the sacred paths we travel. In nature, I can surrender to the unknown. I can rest my mind and bring peace to my soul as I continue to serve others, knowing that all is as it is meant to be. It is here that I can reconnect to Mother Earth's sustaining energy; it recharges and heals me as I continue to navigate these uncertain times.

Gifts

The warmth of sunlight comforts the soul.
The cool earth beneath my feet brings joy.
The strength of towering green trees carries me when I cannot.
The smell of an ocean breeze washes away all cares.
The height of the tallest mountain reminds me that my worries are not as great as I perceive.
The life that surrounds me soothes and heals.
Nature's gifts to all.

Rita Romito-DiGiacomo

BS, BSN, RN, PCCN, Caritas Coach®

Cardiac RN, Cleveland Clinic
Ohio

Rita is a Registered Nurse at Cleveland Clinic Fairview Hospital in Cleveland, Ohio where she has been working as a cardiac nurse for her entire 15 year career. Her practice is grounded in Watson's Theory of Human Caring and Caring Science and she recently became a Caritas Coach®. Before becoming a nurse, she worked as a research scientist at Case Western Reserve University primarily in the field of Neuroscience, working on diseases such as Alzheimer's and Multiple Sclerosis. Rita has always been drawn and connected to Nature and enjoys walking in the beauty and stillness of the outdoors, collecting Nature's treasures, and gardening. She is a creative soul and enjoys making jewelry, writing poetry, drawing/coloring, and above all, making beautiful memories with her husband, John, and two children, Antonia and Gianluca.

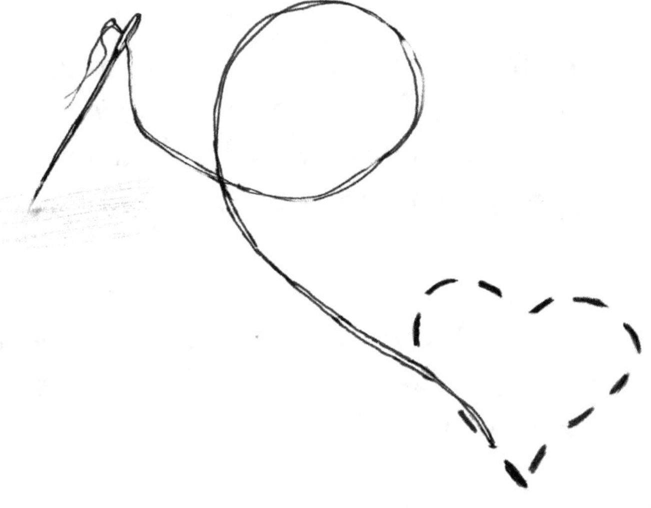

References

Allard, S. (22020, September 23). Who was Patanjali and what are the Yoga Sutras? *Hindu American Foundation*. https://www.hinduamerican. org/blog/who-was-patanjali-and-what-are-the-yoga-sutras/

Arrien, A. (1993). *The Four-Fold Way: Walking the Paths of the Warrior, Teacher, Healer, and Visionary*. HarperOne.

Bolen-Shinoda, J. (2010). Gather the Women. In S. Marohn (Ed.), *Goddess Shift: Women Leading for a Change* (pp. 23–29). Elite Books.

Brown, B. (2021). *Atlas of the Heart: Mapping Meaningful Connection and the Language of Human Experience* (First Edition). Random House.

Brumbaugh Jacobsen, M. (2006). Out of the
mists: An organic inquiry into sacred ways
of knowing and the shaping of reality
[ProQuest Information & Learning (US)].
In *Dissertation Abstracts International
Section A: Humanities and Social Sciences*
(Vol. 67, Issues 5-A, p. 1765). https://
www.proquest.com/docview/621576722/
B630439FF25148BEPQ/1

Combs, A. (2009). *Consciousness Explained
Better: Towards an Integral Understanding of
the Multifaceted Nature of Consciousness.*
Paragon House.

Cowling, W. R., Smith, M. C., & Watson, J. (2008).
The power of wholeness, consciousness,
and caring a dialogue on nursing science,
art, and healing. *ANS. Advances in Nursing
Science*, 31(1), E41-51. https://doi.
org/10.1097/01.ANS.0000311535.11683.d1

Deslauriers, D. (2020). *Heart knowing, somatic
dreaming, and transsubjectivity: A scholarly
personal narrative* [Unpublished Manuscript].
Transformative Inquiry Department,

California Institute of Integral Studies.

Halldorsdottir, S. (1991). Five basic modes of being with another. *NLN Publications, 15–2401*, 37–49.

Hanh, T. N. (2017). *The Other Shore: A New Translation of the Heart Sutra with Commentaries* (Revised ed.). Palm Leaves Press.

Harjo, J. (2021). *Poet Warrior: A Memoir.* W. W. Norton & Company.

Hills, M., Watson, J., & Chantal, C. (2020). *Creating a Caring Science Curriculum, Second Edition: A Relational Emancipatory Pedagogy for Nursing* (2nd edition). Springer Publishing Company.

Merriam-Webster Dictionary. (2022). *Definition of ALCHEMY.* https://www.merriam-webster.com/dictionary/alchemy

Newman, M. A., Smith, M. C., Pharris, M. D., & Jones, D. (2008). The focus of the discipline revisited. *ANS. Advances in Nursing Science*, 31(1), E16-27. https://doi.org/10.1097/01.ANS.0000311533.65941.f1

Reed, S. M. (2010). A unitary-caring conceptual model for advanced practice nursing in palliative care. *Holistic Nursing Practice*, 24(1), 23–34. https://doi.org/10.1097/HNP.0b013e3181c8e4c7

Reed, S. M. (2011). *Experiences in providing and receiving massage and simple touch at the\ end-of-life* [Doctoral dissertation, University of Colorado]. ProQuest Dissertations Publishing

Reed, S. M., Smith, M. C., & Kutner, J. S. (2021). Experiences of Caring Through Providing Touch Near End-of-Life. *International Journal for Human Caring*, 25(2), 142–155. https://doi.org/10.20467/HumanCaring-D-20-00020

Smith, M. C. (1999). Caring and the science of unitary human beings. *ANS. Advances in Nursing Science*, 21(4), 14–28.

Smith, M. C. (2013). Caring and the discipline of nursing. In M. C. Smith, M. C. Turkel, & Z. R. Wolf (Eds.), *Caring in Nursing Classics: An Essential Resource*. Springer Publishing Company.

Smith, M. C., & Reed, S. M. (2007, October). *Toward a Unitary Theory of Healing Through Touch*. Rogerian Scholars Conference, Case Western, Cleveland, Ohio.

Smith, M. C., & Reed, S. M. (2008). Developing a theory of healing through touch. *Journal for Human Caring*, 3(12), 99.

Taylor, J. (1983). *Dream Work: Techniques for Discovering the Creative Power in Dreams* (annotated edition). Paulist Press.

Watson, J. (1985). *Nursing: The Philosophy and Science of Caring*. University Press of Colorado.

Watson, J. (1999). *Postmodern Nursing and Beyond* (1st ed.). Churchill Livingstone.

Watson, J. (2005). *Caring Science as Sacred Science* (1st ed.). F.A. Davis Company.

Watson, J. (2008). *Nursing: The Philosophy and Science of Caring, Revised Edition.* University Press of Colorado.

Watson, J. (Director). (2015, April 27). *Welcome to Human Caring.* The Watson Caring Science Institute. https://www.youtube.com/watch?v=rGv_hDJetYI

Watson, J. (2018). *Unitary Caring Science: Philosophy and Praxis of Nursing* (1st ed). University Press of Colorado.

Watson, J. (2021). *Caring Science as Sacred Science.* Lotus Library.

Watson, J. (2022). Revisiting "Discipline" in Relation to Caring Science as Sacred Science: Revisiting Discipline of Nursing. *Journal of Holistic Nursing: Official Journal of the American Holistic Nurses' Association, 40*(1), 58–63. https://doi.org/10.1177/08980101211041187

Watson, J., Malkin, G., & Alvarez, D. (2005). *The Caring Moment*. In Care for the Journey: Messages and Music for Sustaining the Heart of Healthcare. Wisdom of the World.

Watson Caring
Science Institute

Watson Caring Science Institute is an international non-profit 501C(3) organization that advances the unitary philosophies, theories and practices of 'Caring Science', developed by Dr. Jean Watson. Caring Science is a transdisciplinary approach that incorporates the art and science of nursing and includes concepts from the fields of philosophy, ethics, ecology and mind-body-spirit medicine.

There are an estimated 400 hospitals throughout the USA, in which their professional practice model is based upon Watson's philosophy and theory of human caring science. The institute has trained over 500 Caritas Coaches® globally to translate caring science theory into concrete human-to-human practices that help to repattern the culture of healthcare, whereby the practitioners 'live out' the theory in their professional and personal lives.

Focusing on research, education, practice, and leadership, Watson Caring Science Institute aims to deepen the development and understanding of Caring Science and Caritas Practices, to dramatically transform patient/family experiences of caring and healing in schools, hospitals, the wider community and our planet.

About Lotus Library

Lotus Library is a publication imprint of Watson Caring Science Institute. Following from the philosophy of Caring Science, Lotus Library aims to encompass and showcase a humanitarian, human science orientation to human caring processes, phenomena and experiences. Our mission is rooted in compassionate care and healing of the mind-body-spirit as one. Our publications exemplify a transdisciplinary approach to sustaining caring/healing as a global covenant with humanity/Mother Earth. Lotus Library provides a forum for nurses and others to give voice to phenomena which otherwise may be ignored or dismissed, celebrating the mysteries of life, death suffering and joy, embracing the miracles of existence.

**Jean Watson, PhD, RN, AHN-BC, FAAN, LL (AAN)
Distinguished Professor/Dean Emerita CU Denver
CO, USA. Founder Watson Caring Science Institute**

Dr. Jean Watson is Distinguished Professor and Dean
Emerita, University of Colorado Denver, College of
Nursing Anschutz Medical Center campus, where she
held the nation's first endowed Chair in Caring Science
for 16 years. She is founder of the original Center for
Human Caring in Colorado and is a Fellow of the
American Academy of Nursing; past President of
the National League for Nursing; founding member
of International Association in Human Caring and
International Caritas Consortium. She is Founder and
Director of the non-profit foundation, Watson Caring
Science Institute (www.watsoncaringscience.org). In
2013 Dr. Watson was inducted as a Living Legend by
the American Academy of Nursing, its highest honor.

Her global work has resulted in her being awarded 16 Honorary Doctoral Degrees, 13, international.

Dr. Watson's caring philosophy and theory, including the 10 Caritas Processes® is used to guide transformative models of caring education and professional practices for hospitals, nurses, patients, and communities worldwide. As author / co-author of over 30 books on caring, her latest books range from empirical measurements and international research on caring, mindful caring science practices, to new provocative postmodern philosophies of caring and healing, to advance global caring literacy. Her books seek to bridge paradigms as well as point toward transformative models for this 21st century.

Sean M. Reed

Dr. Sean M. Reed is a board-certified Clinical Nurse Specialist in Adult Health, Hospice and Palliative Care, and Holistic Nursing. As an Assistant Professor at the University of Colorado, College of Nursing, he shares his knowledge and experience with students in the PhD and DNP programs. His research and scholarship are focused on high-value based care in nursing and unitary caring science, which demonstrate his passion for advancing the Discipline. He is recognized for his contributions as a Fellow of the Clinical Nurse Specialist Institute and as a Scholar of the Global Academy of Holistic Nursing. He values the importance of compassionate and holistic approaches to healing, and integrates a philosophy of unitary caring praxis into his life.

Other books in the Series

In English:

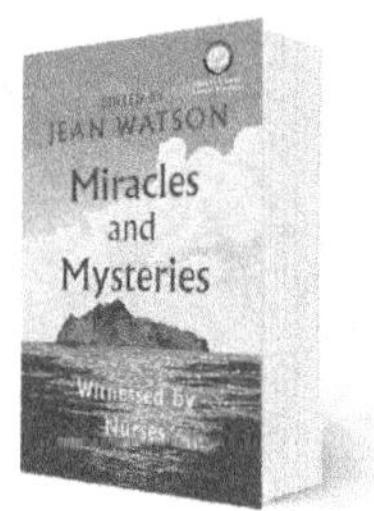

Miracles and Mysteries Witnessed by Nurses, edited by Jean Watson

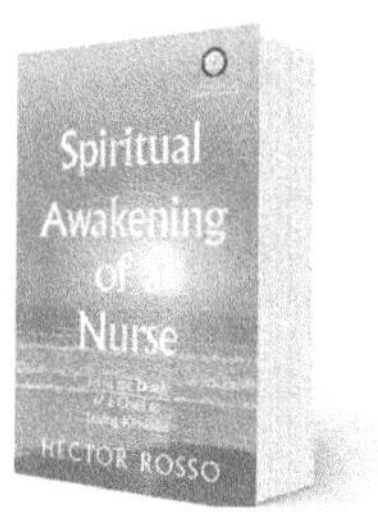

Spiritual Awakening of a Nurse, from the death of a child to loving kindness by Héctor Rosso

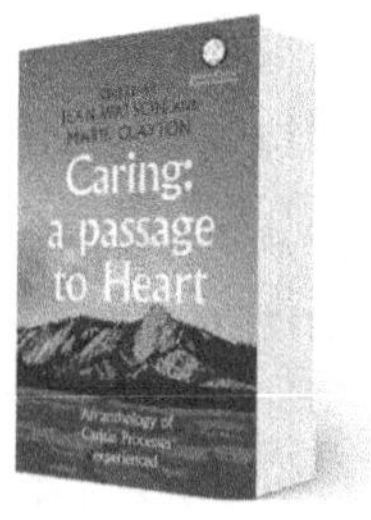

Caring a Passage to Heart, an anthology of caritas processes ® *experienced* edited by Jean Watson and Marie Clayton

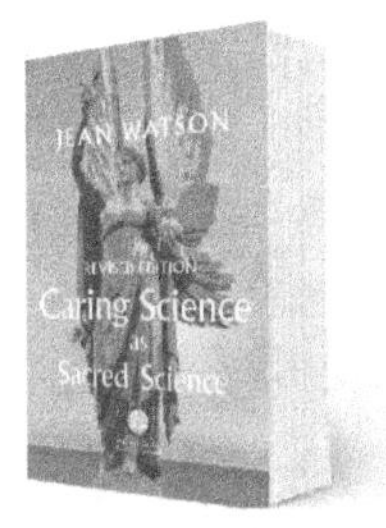 *Caring Science as Sacred Science,* by Jean Watson

In Spainsh:

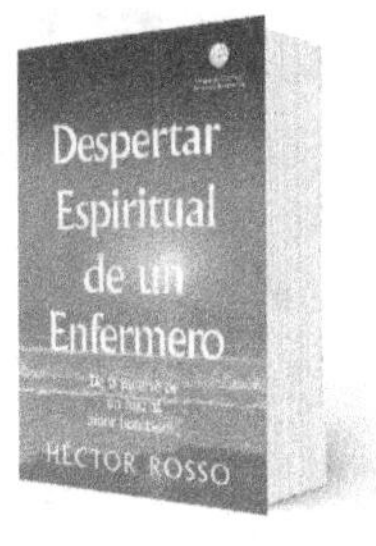 *El Despertar Espiritual de un Enfermero: de la muerte de un hijo al amor bondadoso,* por Héctor Rosso

 *Milagros y Misterios,* Editado por Héctor Rosso, Erika Cabellero, Luana Tonin

www.ingramcontent.com/pod-product-compliance
Lightning Source LLC
Chambersburg PA
CBHW070523160726
48003CB00004B/1677